WELCOME to the BiG KiDS CLUB

What Every Older Sibling Needs to Know!

Words by CHELSEA CLINTON

Pictures by TANIA DE REGIL

PHILOMEL

PHILOMEL BOOKS
An imprint of Penguin Random House LLC, New York

First published in the United States of America by Philomel Books,
an imprint of Penguin Random House LLC, 2022

Visit us online at penguinrandomhouse.com.

Library of Congress Cataloging-in-Publication Data is available.

Printed in the USA

ISBN 9780593350737

10 9 8 7 6 5 4 3 2 1

PC

Edited by Jill Santopolo
Design by Ellice M. Lee
Text set in Bell MT Pro

Art was done in watercolor, acrylic, colored pencil, and Photoshop.

For Charlotte, Aidan,
Jasper and all future big
siblings everywhere
—C. C.

For Aleksander
—T. D. R.

BiG KiDS CLUB

Congratulations!

We heard a new baby is going to be part of your family! That means
you're about to join the Big Kids Club! Being a big sibling is an
important job, and we want to make sure you're prepared. So here's
the Big Kid's Guide to Knowing Your Baby. It's what we wish we had
known before our babies arrived. Are you ready?

Can my baby see me?

All babies are different, and not all of them are born being able to see.

But if your baby can see, everything they see that's not right in front

of them is blurry—so get close and make all the funny faces you want!

If your baby can't see, you can make them laugh using different senses.

Even babies that can see can't see any colors at first, not even the ones

in this book! But in a few months, those babies will be able to focus on

you from the far side of their crib—and see you in color!

Can my baby hear me?

Most babies can hear right away! If your baby can hear, then talk, sing, read, make silly sounds, whistle—whatever you want to do, because most babies love listening to sounds. Nothing too loud, though. That can scare your baby. (If that happens, singing quiet songs might help calm them down.) If your baby can't hear, you can still talk and sing to them while you're holding them so they can feel the vibrations of your voice. You can also communicate with them using your hands.

Why does my baby sleep
all the time?

Newborn babies sleep a lot and don't know the difference between day and night. You can help them with a nighttime routine—maybe just like yours!—so they start to learn to sleep more at night. Maybe you can help with a bath or sing a song you like to hear before you go to sleep. You could even tell them a story.

What does it mean
when my baby cries?

Babies cry for lots of different reasons—
because they're hungry or tired or need a
diaper change or a burp. Sometimes babies
cry because they need a cuddle, and lots
of babies cry when they're getting new
teeth. They won't stop when you ask them
to, even if you say please. But as you get
to know your baby, you'll learn what's
making them cry and how you can help
your grown-up make your baby feel better.

What does my baby eat?

Some babies eat breast milk and some babies eat formula—and that's usually all they eat for the first six months. After that, your baby might start to drink plain water or eat really mushed-up soft foods. For their first birthday, they might get to eat cake! (You might get a piece, too.)

Why does my baby need to burp?

Lots of babies swallow air when they eat (some big kids and grown-ups do, too). All that air can hurt your baby's tummy and make them fussy. To help them get rid of the air, your grown-up will burp your baby. That's what all the back rubbing and tapping is for! They might even let you help—but be sure to use a burp cloth, if you have one, because some babies spit up when they burp.

Why does my baby poop so much?

Newborn babies eat every two to three hours, and some of them poop after every meal. So, if your baby is a baby who does that, well . . . that's a lot of pooping! As they get older, they'll probably start pooping a little less often. But in the meantime, if you don't mind when things are a little stinky, you can offer to help your grown-up with diaper changes when your baby poops. (And don't worry if your baby's poop looks different than yours; it's because you eat big kid food, and they don't yet.)

When can my baby talk to me?

Not for a while. Maybe when they're a year old? Or maybe a few months earlier or later. Some babies talk much later than that, and some others don't talk at all, or they talk with their hands or the help of a computer. A lot of babies' first words are "dada" or "mama," but if your baby's a big talker, their first words might be something like . . . "Tyrannosaurus rex" or "elephant snorkle" (but probably not).

When can my baby walk?

Like talking, this happens whenever babies are ready, and sometimes not at all. Some babies also to learn to sit up, crawl and stand up. There's so much to do! And you can help them by showing them how it's all done. When your baby can take five steps without falling over, that's considered walking. And if your baby can't walk, there will be other ways for them to get around.

Why do I have to wash my hands
before I touch my baby when
they're brand new?

Just after they're born, your baby won't be able to fight off germs very well. Something that might just give you a little cold could make your baby super sick. It's no fun when your baby gets sick, so make sure you wash your hands or use a hand sanitizer before touching your baby—and make sure anyone else who wants to hold your brand-new baby does the same!

Why wasn't my baby born with teeth?

Babies don't need teeth when they're born because their bodies aren't ready to eat solid food yet. Don't worry, they'll get teeth when they need them to chew food, and it's completely safe for older babies to eat soft food even if they don't have any teeth!

Why do I keep being told to be careful with my baby's head?

Your baby is born with two soft spots on their head—one in the front and one in the back. Over time, their head bones will strengthen, but until then you have to be gentle when you touch anywhere on your baby's head, especially during a bath or if you're helping brush your baby's hair.

Does my baby understand
when I say "I love you"?

Even before your baby understands words, they'll know what it means when someone hugs them, kisses them, smiles at them and makes them laugh. So, while they might not understand what the words "I love you" mean, you can do other things so they know that their big kid loves them so much. And guess what? As soon as they learn how to communicate, they'll probably tell you in their own ways that they love you back.

There's so much to learn about your baby! Like their name, their favorite song, their favorite story and their favorite dance moves! But at least you know one thing for sure: your baby is yours and you'll get to love them forever.